DOIN DIFFERENT:
NEW BALLADS FROM THE EAST OF ENGLAND

Further details of Poppyland Publishing titles can be found at
www.poppyland.co.uk
*where clicking on the 'Support and Resources' button
will lead to pages specially compiled to support this book*

Join us for more Norfolk and Suffolk stories and background at
www.facebook.com/poppylandpublishing

Doin different.

New ballads from the East of England

By Gareth Calway

DEDICATION
TO MELANIE, WITHOUT WHOM . . .

I AM GRATEFUL BEYOND WORDS FOR ALL THE MUSIC, PHOTOGRAPHS, PERFORMANCE ART, FILM, PROMOTION AND PERSONAL SUPPORT FROM THE FRIENDS AND FELLOW ARTISTS WHO HAVE CONTRIBUTED SO GENEROUSLY TO THIS BOOK.

Copyright © 2015 Gareth Calway

First published 2015 by Poppyland Publishing, Cromer, NR27 9AN

www.poppyland.co.uk

ISBN 978-1-909796-22-5

Designed and typeset in Cambria 14pt on 16.5 pt

Printed by Lightning Source

Picture credits

Barry Allan pp. 21, 31, 41, 105

Author pp. 56-57

Tim Chipping p. 68

Jo Conway p. 95

Ron Fiske Collection p. 71

Courtesy of Lynn News p. 27

Vince Matthews p. 23

John McClennan 101

Anto Morra pp. 32, 59. 69, 84, 85, 91, 97

Tony Rafferty pp. 13, 40, 73

Mike Page p. 17

Percy Paradise Back cover

Roger Partridge p. 63

Poppyland Collection pp. 64, 87

Poppyland Photos pp. 14-15, 29, 30, 39, 44, 47, 49, 52, 55, 88, 92, 93, 94

Al Pulford Photography 37

SHARP pp. 16, 20, 50-51

Joan Tebbutt p. 106

Joan Wall p. 75

Zariah Wood Davies Cover, pp. 2, 35

Emma Withington p. 11

Thanks to Chris Duarte of St George's Music Shop, Norwich, for printing and editing the music scores.

Contents

Publisher's Note

We'd really like to have made this a fully interactive book – print, music, words, video, pints of beer – but the world isn't quite ready yet. But as with many Poppyland Publishing books, we'd like to give you access to many more resources linked to the title – there are lots of them!

Go to www.poppyland.co.uk and click on the 'Support and Resources' button - or use this QR code - and you'll find the book cover and further links to Gareth's Blogspot, musicians' pages, gig lists and video links for the ballads – and let us know if you post performances of the ballads you'd like included on the link.

Foreword

I was glad to be asked by Gareth Calway to write a short introduction to his new book "Doin different", or a history of Norfolk from Boudicca to Edith Cavell in ballad form. Recalling the definition of the latter I found: "Ballad. Properly a song to be danced to but from the 16th c. or earlier the term has been applied to anything singable, simple, popular in style, and for solo voice". Such singers were also ballad sellers hawking their broadsheets on contemporary events or the human condition. Urban streets, market places and public houses were all locations.

With the onset of mass printing by the 17th c. the number of ballad singers in England increased. They became part of a rich cultural tradition with ballads springing from the experience of the common people. Gareth Calway's ballad book owes most to this oral history. Indeed, he tells us that his writing is for the folk clubs/pubs audience, and for musicians to set and sing.

It is pleasing to see West Norfolk well represented in the book but the ballads take us across our exceptional county, from Lynn to Yarmouth, Cromer to Thetford, and on to Norwich and UEA. And his chosen people and events span about a thousand years. I like the ballad about the Cod Fishers or "homage to an unsung and underpaid group of East Anglian heroes" who sailed to Iceland for cod in Tudor and Stuart times to feed the nation. At least 111 ships left the region's harbours in 1593 for the North Atlantic. Of special interest for me too is the ballad of Badass King John who lost his "dosh" in the Wash after leaving Lynn in October 1216. In the thriving Wash port he was not regarded as so bad but "a gallant little Linnet King". Then there is Mother Julian, Margery Kempe, Kett, Cromwell, Walpole, Fanny Burney, Townshend and Tom Paine as well as the Peasants' Revolt.

I am sure these ballads will attract attention, not least because the book will also be the hub of a multi media package of filmed performances and recordings. Having attended dynamic live performances of Gareth's group in Lynn on Cromwell, Margery Kempe and Sawtre, I also believe these ballads will capture new audiences for our "shared" East Anglian heritage, of the story of Norfolk and England. Whether they will be pasted on pub walls as in the past I don't know – today, that would be "Doin different!"

Dr Paul Richards FSA DL.
Lynn

Author's Introduction

Wordsworth's collaborator on 'Lyrical Ballads', ST Coleridge, famously defined poetry as 'the best words in the best order.' But what about the music, Sam? Aren't ballads supposed to have music? Anyone who has joined in a ballad chorus will know what music adds even to 'the best words in the best order.'

Music enacts the heart's story beating through the words. Singing them exposes any pretentiousness in the lyric. When Wordsworth in the preface to his Lyrical Ballads prefers 'real' language to 'artifice', I think this is what he means.

The ballad metre is glorious in its simplicity, has endured for a millennium and become an instinct in the English speaking world. (Ironic that it began as a courtly French form.) It's not the only metre but it is the high road, or rather the well-beaten track over common ground: equally familiar in pop songs, hymns, cards and (written down differently) the blues. It's all about the beat. The most common written convention and the one I have mostly followed is the quatrain rhymed ABCB, with four beats to the unrhymed line and three to the rhymed. The rhyme clinches the thought of the stanza: a glib rhyme or a vague/failed concept exposed by a good one, and you are lost. An exact syllable count of 8 and 6 adds a purist precision – good ballads have the modernist virtues of economy and concreteness and these especially so - but no matter how many syllables, the 4/3 beat count drives the lines. This supreme version of the ballad form when handled well has generated a seemingly inexhaustible variety of classic ballads but the complete Child Ballads include other popular variants which share its principles of distilled simplicity; common humanity; fate, earth, air, fire and water; a cleared mind and a beating heart.

Ballads tell a cracking story in verse. History, Ghosts, Murders, Legends, Outlaws, Love, Tragedy. Man and Woman against the elements and odds. Underdogs against the top dogs. Robin Hood ballads tell the story of the poor against the barons and contain much more social realism than 'courtly' art forms. In real life his merry men ('companions') were only 'merry' in the original meaning ('short-lived') and while there is folktale-romance in the forest setting, and Robin's frequent triumphs, the real mediaeval world in all its gore and savage punitive laws is viscerally seen from the bottom of society up, all the way to his realistic end. The ballad, then, is the underdog's tale but there are many kinds of underdog, even Robin's King John, who intriguingly attracts more sympathy in ballads than in Good King Richard/Bad King John 'histories'.

Ballads are down in the earth, where the workers are. Were the old ballads 'folk' compositions, then, a collective enterprise like sailing a ship? Romantic scholars writing in Victorian libraries thought so, and pushed the date of composition back into a remote 'folk' past. But while the oldest, 'Judas,' is 12th c. and ballad metre is early mediaeval in origin, the golden age of ballad writing is actually from the time of the Civil War peaking in the Enlightenment age of Walpole and written by professional minstrels. So this view of ballad composition as a 'folk' activity has been dismissed.

But hold you hard on that condescension. The average football or political chant is rarely the work of a professional minstrel. (Carrow Road's 'On The Ball' - that official paean in praise of attacking adventure, 'never mind the danger' – may be the exception that proves the rule here.) The football crowd is a Greek Chorus of folk creativity – reworking popular songs, adverts, hymns, carols with menacing wit, collective emotion, primitive energy, a stamping communal beat and a frequently unacknowledged level of sophistication, both musical and verbal. Ferocious fans sing together in public at the top of their lungs – hold a tune; keep a beat; sing their hearts out for joy; snarl in shared despair; accompany and orchestrate themselves with drums, trumpets, hand claps, feet stomps. If the crowd doesn't join in with the bellowed improvisation, the individual will want the terrace to open up and swallow him or her like a mid-match pie and it probably will. But if it's taken up, it will spread to other terraces the next week, in ever-new variants.

The ballad lyric retains this folk dynamic. It is definitely 'of the people' and while rarely *written* collectively, its public character still decides the way an individual poet like myself writes in it. I am writing these words for the folk club/pub audience and for musicians to set and sing: addressing a shared East Anglian/ English heritage, telling our bit of the island story from Boudicca to Cavell. Please join in!

This book came about as a result of my love of the ballad form, the rich history of this region and music. The ballads began life as poems that can be enjoyed on the page and read aloud. Then as I became more involved with the local folk scene I became aware of the abundance and variety of talent and creativity in our folk clubs. Unable to compose music myself but a life-long wordsmith, I realised that many musicians were composing tunes but often needed words. I am more than happy to supply them. And so came the idea of a book that could provide a resource for musicians. I approached several to have a go at doing a ballad just as a sample of what could be done. I was astounded by the response. The profusion, quality and variety of contributions were remarkable and testimony to the creativity in our folk clubs. Many of the ballads in this book have links to performances (both film and audio) of the songs. A few have musical scores or just guitar chords. Some ballads have been covered by different artists, showing how the same lyrics can be used to create very different effects. So this book can be enjoyed in a variety of ways; just immerse yourself in the words that tell the stories of our area; follow the links to see how they have been read aloud, acted or set to music; and if inspired to write your own tunes then go forth and perform them.

Gareth Calway
November 2015
www.garethcalway.co.uk

1. The Ballad of Fiddler's Hill [1]

Ye feasters up on Fiddler's Hill
Where crossroads meet the harrow,
Take care you don't disturb the sleeping
Bronze Age burial barrow.

O shun this ground from dusk to dawn
Or live a dreadful tale
Of a Black Monk at the tunnel's mouth
To turn your red lips pale.

Don't follow the fiddler and his dog
To Walsingham under the hill
To lay the foul Benedictine ghost:
That fiddler lays there still.

"I will play through the tunnel!" cried the jolly fiddler
To the cheering local crowd,
"Stamp time and follow my tune above,
For I play both brave and loud."

And so he fiddled and so they stamped
His three mile course underground
But his fiddle stopped under Fiddler's Hill
In the silence of the mound.

Each dared the next down the tunnel's mouth
But none would dare themselves
And at midnight the fiddler's dog emerged
Like a hound bewitched of the elves.

His tail thrust down between his legs,
His frame a shivering wrack,
He howled and pined at the dreadful hole
But his master never came back.

---

[1]   Legend has it that a tunnel runs from Binham Priory to Walsingham and only a person brave enough to walk it can lay its dreadful ghost - a Priory monk. A brave fiddler took up the challenge, the sound of his fiddle followed above ground by local folk. The music stopped under the Bronze Age barrow.

"I will play through the tunnel!" cried the jolly fiddler
To the cheering local crowd,
"Stamp time and follow my tune above,
For I play both brave and loud."

A violent storm drove everyone home
And when they awoke from sleep
The entrance was gone, the fiddler too,
Into a Nameless Deep.

In this county of beet and barley and beer,
This county of fish and farrow,
There's folk you can trust, there's London folk,
And there's folk who come out of a barrow.

The moral of this, and it's old as the hill,
Is that mounds aren't for tunnelling,
If a grave tune plucks the strings of your heart,
Keep the devil under your chin.

"I will play through the tunnel!" cried the jolly fiddler
And half his boast came true,
"Stamp time and follow my tune above!"
But he lost them half way through.

Gareth and the Fried Pirates on Fiddler's Hill.

11

The Ballad of Fiddler's Hill

Gareth Calway

Gill Sims McLennan

The full score for The Ballad of Fiddler's Hill is on page 102.

2. The Ballad of Boudica

She is history not myth but remember
History is written by the vicar
And she neither wrote nor won.
No freedom, no future, no fun.

Rome had to win or lose an Empire,
Britain had to win or simply expire,
And with it the Western horizon,
No freedom, no future, no fun.

Procurator Decianus Catus
Spoke down his nose, spoke down his anus,
"The Emperor claims the dead king's kingdom"
No freedom, no future, no fun.

There's no future in your Roman dream,
Your traffic lanes and your shopping schemes,
Your soapless baths and your manly steam,
The Iceni queen bee is making free
With your city!

She danced to the wardrums, warhooves, hornwhine,
Exhorting, as Romans were drilled into line,
Her race to fling back the squares of London:
No freedom, no future, no fun.

Now her rebels hole up, where home is none,
On roots thin as hope and a dream of Britain,
Hunted through nettles and thorns, their soles stung:
No freedom, no future, no fun.

Her hard core Iceni's last stand and fall
Is the longest, fiercest, stubbornest of all
But is crushed - like flint - in The Battle of Thornham:
No freedom, no future, no fun.

There's no future in your Roman dream,
Your traffic lanes and your shopping schemes,
Your soapless baths and your manly steam,
The Iceni queen bee is making free
With your city!

"Our Roman matrons have a place too
In a civilised home: I could offer you
A place in mine: dresses, baths, decorum:"
No freedom, no future, no fun.

Death-and-glory queens, country dragons:
Whores of fashion in Camolodunum,
In Roman roses their own scent gone,
No freedom, no future, no fun.

The salts that she sowed in the Squareheads' wounds
Return in a wash that will sour our lands
But they couldn't chain her to the History of Rome:
She chariots a tide in Whitehall home.

There's no future in your Roman dream,
Your traffic lanes and your shopping schemes,
Your soapless baths and your manly steam,
The Iceni queen bee is making free
With your city!

3. The Ballad of The Bagaudae (The Body In The Oven)

"The cremation appears to have been the final event on the site – performed when the oven was already crumbling...the latest coin being an issue of Magnentius (AD 350-353) ... The treatment of the body (in the oven) (appears) less than respectful...(it may be) an attempt to dispose the body of someone who had been murdered... One possibility is ... bagaudae... rural social bandits whose resistance to the authority of state and the landlords occasionally swelled into a full scale peasants' revolt" (Digging Sedgeford. A people's archaeology pp. 64-6.) Unless (as one SHARP participant observes) it was suicide!"

"Ah, no; the years O!

How the sick leaves reel down in throngs." (Thomas Hardy)

> Their grain drying ovens, their malting floors,
> Stone-rusting apart at the seams;
> Their pottery, glass beads and finger rings
> Are flashes that pyre-light a stream.
>
> Iron soldiers and landlords, collectors of tax,
> Stone villas and forts and towns,
> Summer laurels and oak leaves of gleaming green
> Stalked helpless and withered and brown.
>
> By tax, rent and debt, tax, rent and labour,
> The poor give their meek to the rich,
> *Pax Romana* – an army; its *civitas* – towns
> And villas we farm in a ditch.
>
> *What once was an oven to fire clay and grain,*
> *Keep the blaze of their 'civitas' burning*
> *Is now the hot grave of this landowning thief,*
> *This agent of Rome - and worms turning.*[2]

2   In performance, repeat this chorus after every verse. Civitas means 'civilisation'

The remarkable excavations at Sedgeford continue on an annual basis.

4. The Ballad of Sedgeford

This is the most primary-sourced ballad in this book. It interprets three traumatised skulls excavated from fields near my home by archaeologists on the Sedgeford Historical and Archaelogical Research Project, SHARP.

He came from the north and he killed my kin
And I curse him with my bones;
Cuthbert and Carl confronted him
For their husband-hood and homes.

Cuthbert was kingly, stood strong and straight
And he spoke the stranger fair,
'Wanderer, you're welcome to fire and food
But your seax stays out there.'

'Brave words for a bondsman, no soldier you,
Your nose and knuckles unbroken!'
'We are farmers and freemen,' called Carl at his shoulder,
His axe held a threat unspoken.

'Who's the milksop behind ye?' the stranger spat
And Carl's face blushed with blood,
Cuthbert restrained him with kingly hand,
Then grovelled into the mud.

A hack from the heel had hobbled his ham,
Broken his pride at the knee;
Another shattered his jaw from his head,
No face any longer had he.

Carl hoisted axe like a hulk to an oak
But it heaved a blade of its own,
Crowned Carl like a cowering coney caught
In the hole of its hearth and home.

'Meet the thegn of your village, hall, ovens, gate,
You're now all working for me!
The run of the mill, port, sedge, ford and stream
And defences I oversee.'

He cut off Carl's head from its grounded corpse,
Held it high for the village to see.
'Wench with that stone-in-a-tooth of a frown
Like a sore nagging nerve, take heed!'

He heaved off Carl's ear and threw it at me,
Took Cuthbert's and did the same,
'Knit me a necklace of killed coward ears,
Then tell me your pretty name.'

'Carl was my blood-kin; I'm Cuthbert's wife
By priest and the Christian God.'
'Bring me this priest and his high-throat, by Thor,
I'll throttle and throw to my dog.'

'We serve the monastery up on the hill'
The priest said, his high voice lost
In the thundering laughter of Seax the Dane,
'By my village it will be bossed!'

The Cuthbert-folk came up from river, from woods,
From oven-sheds and smelting,
From barley and wheat-fields, sheep-hill and plot,
From kitchens and chapel praying.

'In these dread doubtful days of burning barns,
Of monastery ovens raided,
I will head you, protect you, *my* weald on the Wash
Will never be invaded.'

'Now wench, to the bed of your master and mate!'
The priest kneeled - and begged his mercy,
'But widows must mourn and women must choose
The master they will marry.'

Thegn Seax the Dane had an answer that had
The little priest thinking double,
A blade to the brain in a broken skull
To thank him for his trouble.

I buried my kin as East as guess gets
At night in the ancient boneyard
And tended our priest for four raving weeks
Till he took his bark to the stars.

Now I serve my master Seax the Dane
In a life that has lost all reason
And his steaming oysters and coneys I cook -
And with nightshade daily season.

Cuthbert and Carl confronted him
For their husband-hood and homes;
He came from the north and he killed my kin
And I curse him with their bones.

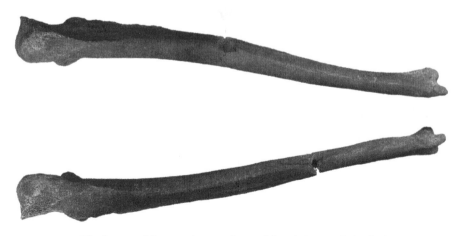

The fractured forearm bones of one of the victims at Sedgeford.

Bob Bones with the author

5. Lancelot And The Grail Maiden

'But all my heart is drawn above
My knees are bowed in crypt and shrine:
I never felt the kiss of love,
Nor maiden's hand in mine.'
Tennyson, Sir Galahad.

'Come hither, Captain,' the Grail Maiden sighs,
'Come thither away with me
To the rich wooded valley and holy well
My Waste Land dies to be.

'Look! into the burning wilderness sun
Above the shadeless tree,
The high hawk of summer, hovering still,
The shadow of what will be:

'The Shadowless One who waits above
To be born to you and me,
A Knight of Truth out of traitor arms
And infidelity.

'Galahad the Pure, God-armed and winged
To bless our impurity
Unbearably born to steal your quest
And all of your shining glory.

'Come hither, Captain,' the Grail Maiden sighs,
And turns him a face so free:
His forbidden love, the queen of his dreams,
The end of all Chivalry.'

A faithless false knight in a failing light
Fallen under a spell to see
A Knight of Truth out of traitor arms
And infidelity.

Says he, 'My heart is set on the grail
And wholly raised above!'
Says she, 'It's broken, and half is set
On your true adulterous love.'

'I am her champion, she is my king's,
I am their faithful knight!'
'The Grail can't be had for half a heart,
You can have that queen tonight.

*'Whisper my name, any name you like,
Any lover you want me to be,
A night of Truth in my traitor arms
And in fidelity.'* [3]

Vince Matthews.

[3]   Alfred Lawn Tennyson's idylls of King Arthur's knights and winsome ladies aren't actually set among the barley sheaves and manor houses of his native Lincolnshire but they seem to haunt them. Arthurian romance may be understood historically as an idealised memory of Celtic and Roman civilisations absorbed through Brittany by Norman knights seeking ancient British precedents to legitimise their courtly love quests and their conquest of Angle-land. Or not. CS Lewis says of that twelfth century Tennyson Chretien de Troyes, 'It is interesting to notice that he places his ideal in the past. For him already "the age of chivalry is dead." It always was: let no-one think the worse of it on that account. These phantom periods for which the historian searches in vain... have their place in a history more momentous than that which commonly bears the name.' (CS Lewis. 'The Allegory of Love OUP. 1958. P.23-24)

6. The Ballad Of A Twelfth Century Hood

It was on a somer's evening,
The merry month of May,
When buds are free and briddes sing
And leaves are brave and gay.

I met a surly abbot,
Cruel steward at his side
And now his guards lay slain or fled
But at me he did chide,

'Pawn so soiled and churlish,
Living like a beast,
Your king crusades against the Turk,
Spare me and join the feast."

"Norman," I laughed, your danelaw's
Ploughed every inch of this land,
You've snatched your danegeld twice and thrice
With chainmail on your hand,"

"Now stubborn as Danish sokeman
And true as Saxon thegn
With a 'waes heal' and a freeman's shout,
We snatch it back again.

"In the name of good King Alfred
And the nation that he saved,
In the Lincoln green of an English knight,
We make our own crusade."

"There's knight blood on my longstaff
Fresh as the day I fled:
I hit him and hit him and hit him
And hit him until he was dead.

I'm much too far gone, Abbot,
For you to save my soul,
Besides in that great pile of flesh,
Where's yours? The devil's hole.

"For all your noble churches
With turrets and with towers,
For all your royal forest laws
The venison is ours.

"Call for beef and mutton,
It tastes like sheep and cow,
Stuff your pork till you're blue in the face,
It's villein's boar and sow.

"You can keep your cuckoo's feathers,
Your fancy foreign drawl,
All we want back is the silver and gold
You loot by cross and law.

"In the name of good King Alfred
And the nation that he saved,
In the Lincoln green of an English knight,
We make our own crusade."

The swift as the sunlight's flicker
Behind the still-leafed tree,
I caught the chink of a tinkling spur
And a mounted lady's plea.

"Stout yeman, I beg your mercy
Upon yon abbot's life,"
Golden hair flowed from her golden crown,
In my heart went a long cold knife.

"She'd never meant to parley
Though she used the English tongue,
You slew a knight whose daughter I am.
Now your bowstring music's sung."

I planted my last arrow
Deep in the forest green,
"Where it lands I live an outlaw forever."
I fell at the feet of my queen.

Now the light is painfully fading
On the merry songs we sang
And the flight for our lives through the trees
And the future left to hang...

"In the name of God's King Alfred
And the harvest that he saved,
Against these king of the castle knights,
We've made our last crusade."[4]

4   Is Robin Hood history, legend, romance, folk tale or myth? All at once though much nearer English history than the time-travelling Arthur whose reign lasts from a Celtic Bronze Age of magical swords to a Tudor memory of Norman shining armour. Here I've just imagined a real Saxon outlaw emerging from the greenwood mists, a locus for the grim social realism and comment that laces the romance of the Robin Hood ballads.

7. The Ballad of Badass King John

The Angevins were Very Bad,
And Worst of All was John:
As foul as hell is, it's defiled
By Eleanor's Little One.

Wicked, selfish, lecherous, cruel,
Insolent, shameless, wrong,
Kin-killing, vicious, spiteful, *French*, (pah!)
Dishonoured, grasping John.

Usurped his Lionhearted Bro,
The One Good Angevin;
Jugged Merry Freeborn *English* (yay!)
Forest-flying Robin.

Villain of the Good/Bad History
School and book and song,
'Inadequate with some Capone'
John. King John. ...Bad King John.

In 1216 at all time low,
His 'soft sword' half advanced,
His shrunk-crown empire Richard-pawned,
Normandy lost to France, (pah!)

Despised by all those Magna barons
Carting him to heel
Flinging him to French invaders
And Abdullah's deal:

England given to Mohammed!
A rock moored off Morocco,
Hapless John at bay and 4 years
Excommunicado.

Villain of the Good/Bad History
School and book and song,
'Inadequate with some Capone'
John. King John. ...Bad King John.

From Lynn, he armied up to Lincoln
As the Wellstream rose[5],
Despised by Emperor, peasant, guild;
His Rome-rule churches closed;

3000 men, wheels coming off,
Up creek without a guide;
The royal dosh lost in the Wash -
He never lost our pride.

For out in Norfolk we do different,
And his haven, it was Lynn,
Their domain he made our borough[6],
Gallant little Linnet king.

Victim of the Good/Bad History
School and book and song,
His Brother's Bad Book Good Book Keeper
John. King John. ...Good King John.

[5] http://www.edp24.co.uk/norfolk-life/norfolk; history/41_king_john_s_treasure_1_214293
[6] http://www.archives.norfolk.gov.uk/view/NCC110530

8. Dissolution Row: The Ballad of Binham Priory

Call their names from the rubble: Alexander de Langley,
Mad as a scholar – 'here'.
William de Somerton, William Dyxwell,
Priors and bad boys - 'here.'

A mad monk in solitary, buried in chains,
Tortured to brake his devil;
Alchemy funded by holy sales,
Double and bubble and trouble;

Monks eating bran and drinking rain
Till King John raised the siege;
A wanderlust prior, administ-truant,
Deposed and then reprieved.

'As the leaves of summer break in spring
From forest, field and tree
So let the song of freedom burst
From the walls of this Priory.'

The peasants were revolting here
In 1381
When Master Lister led the charge
That started all the fun.

'Enough!' he cried, 'of fattened bishops
Fed on Priory rolls,
Enough of tenants, rents and lords
And serfdom's heavy loads.'

'I'll join that fight!' said Binham John Lister
To his name-sake of Felmingham
George whose Norfolk Peasant Spring
Brought mayhem into Binham.

Chorus

The Fightin' Norwich Bishop sniffed
The peasants' merry fire;
The Fightin' Bishop's fist of Christ
Killed it with his ire.

'Lister of Felmingham, for sins against
Your betters and your King,
I'll have your guts for my Bishop's garter
And the serfs can kiss my ring.'

'You can hang my neck and quarter my guts
But my soul flies straight to heaven
When Adam delved and Eve span, 'lord',
What rents were recked in Eden?

Chorus
The old order stood another six generations,
Its dead Norms carved in art
Then the ghost of Lister came back to haunt
The Priory's stony heart.

He laughed as Henry's inspector called,
Found 'fault' with the Priory rolls,
'Down with these rood screens, saints and crowns
And idol Gods on poles;

'Whitewash these saints from the walls of the nave,
A clear new page for the Word,
 Your bishops' bank is ruined now
There are no serfs to herd!

Chorus

This high Notre Dame of Norfolk shrunk
To a nave-sized Parish Church,
Abandoned wings sold off for stone
To men scarce more than serfs

But when Paston quarried the haunted pile
To build a house in the grounds,
 A wall killed a workman and none to this day
Will build in Priory bounds.

Three miles to the West, Roman relics and smoke
Rise again from Celtic Earth
Like the re-appeared saints whose rooted gaze
Reclaims the walls of this church.

'Let the holy rain of autumn fall
From the solitary tree
And the grass grow wild and the four winds blow
Through the grounds of this Priory.'

Julie Bones with Percy Paradise at Folk in a Field

9. The Ballad of Julian of Norwich

"He said not 'Thou shalt not be tempested, thou shalt not be travailed, thou shalt not be dis-eased'; but he said, 'Thou shalt not be overcome...'

'All shall be well and all manner of thing shall be well.'

Mother Julian Revelations of Divine Love.

They buried her alive in here,
The dead they'll never raise
The maid a parish came to love,
A movement came to praise.

No motion has she now, her course
Is inward, grave and still;
The church behind her every move,
The tomb her anchored will.

''So, Julie, can I ask-' A hush.
It's 'Julian' she sighs.
'You after some big bishopric?'
'I need no name that dies.'

'I'm out of here if that's your tale,
My column talks the town.
I'll lose my pitch, my job, my mind,
I've got to nail this down.'

'O frightened child, just run to Him,'
I'm not like you – you're dead!
'Dead to the world yet still attached,
All shall be well,' she said.

'He showed into my mind a nut.'
I'm seeing one, I grin.
'In it we seek its maker, rest
Where there no rest is in.'

'You saw Eternity last May
Through Death's wedged-open door?'
'This crucifix - like rain from eaves,
I saw its hot blood pour.'

'I saw in sixteen shewings how
We must – we can - abide
Dis-ease, travail and storm, for we're
The thorn in God's soft side.

'Which side is that?' *'His female side'*
'The Trinity has another?'
'Christ bears us all upon His breast,
His wound's our womb and mother.

'O frightened child, just run to him,'
I'm not like you – you're dead!
'Dead to the world yet still attached,
All shall be well,' she said.

10. The Ballad of William Sawtrey of Lynn

William Sawtrey of Bishop's Lynn, Margery Kempe's parish priest, was the first heretic to be burned for his beliefs in England. He was charged under the Statute of Heresies (1400), 'examined' by the Bishop of Elmham and burned in London in 1401. Much of 'Lollardy' - a uniquely English heresy - would resurface later as Protestantism. Whether Sawtrey was the first Protestant martyr or the 'Morning Star' (Lucifer) of the English Reformation depends which side of the Eucharistic bread you're on.

"If by this act I can light a flame
Feed the wax of Flesh to burn Love's Name
In the unlettered lives of Jesu's people,
The ground down to earth, the poor, the meek, the faithful:
The pain of Flesh passing is well worth the candle.
It's a heaven to die for!"

(from A Nice Guy: The Burning of William Sawtrey)

William, you're a Lynn boy!
Where's your Norfolk grit?
Your mind is like a frightened girl,
It makes me want to spit.

This is Boudicca's country.
Stand your ground
Like those battered women
Who would not lie down! ...

They told me that the bread became
Christ's Body not His Ghost.
I said a priest's no sorcerer
That did it: I was toast.

They tortured me, 'recant
Your reasoning, or roast!'
I said 'I cannot bear your Cross.'
That did it: I was toast.

They told me that Richeldis saw
Our Lady not a ghost.
I said 'chalk eggs to Falsingham!'
That did it: I was toast.

They said a Roman prayer or Mass
Would keep me in my post.
I said 'An English sermon's best.'
That did it. I was toast.

'Our Sacraments are spirit gold,'
The brassy bishops boast
'And all that gilders isn't God!'
That did it: I was toast.

They Credo-bashed, defrocked and lashed
My body to their post.
I answered them with Balaam's ass.
That did it: I was toast.

They told me that the bread became
The hostage not the host.
I said 'Man needs the bread as well.'
That did it: I was toast.

They burn me like a fallen Eve,
A holy without smoke,
I climb up like a morning star,
The dreamer's gleam of hope.

*William Sawtrey become toast (figuratively speaking) in a
production of 'A Nice Guy' at the Hanse House courtyard,
King's Lynn*

Farewell William

Vanessa Wood-Davies

11. The Ballad of Margery Kempe

I cut a dash through Bishop's Lynn,
Proud daughter of its Mayor,
My cloaks with modish tippets slashed,
And gold pipes in my hair.

I burned to die, I sinned a sin
That's never been confessed
– Except to God – a Lollard sin
To hold it in my breast.

This Book I weep in blood
Up from the heart's deep well
Would drown the earth in heaven tears
And church the tongues of hell.

But hearing heaven's Song of Songs
I shun the gutter's Ouse
And though you rule me, husband, priest,
A single life I choose

And every pilgrim step I trudge
From wedlock's grave mundane
And married flesh and churchman's plot
Is singing with God's name.

This Book I weep in blood
Up from the heart's deep well
Would drown the earth in heaven tears
And church the tongues of hell.

Joanna Swan as Margery

12. The Ballad of Anne Boleyn

Anne Boleyn's ghost is said to haunt Blickling Hall every year on the night of May 19, the anniversary of her execution in 1536. Her first love, the dashing poet and statesman Sir Thomas Wyatt, who watched her die from his own cell in the Tower, was one of six alleged adulterers accused by Henry VIII.

(Wyatt)

A moon of May and a shining hour
Hunted hind harried in the gloom
And passing fair is the fading flower
Fa la la la la la la la la la.

You stalked me softly who later flew
Hunted hind harried in the gloom
And kissed me bold, wild and free and new.
Fa la la la la la la la la la.

With lips of young, sweet and dangerous rose
Hunted hind harried in the gloom
That like the blood-red of summer blows.
Fa la la la la la la la la la.

(Anne Boleyn)

So wild to hold though I seem so tame;
Hunted hind harried in the gloom
I lost my heart when I won the game.
Fa la la la la la la la la la.

A Tudor rose and a May queen's throne.
Hunted hind harried in the gloom
I plucked them both and now both are gone.
Fa la la la la la la la la la.

I lost my soul for a golden band
Hunted hind harried in the gloom
That bows the neck as it forced the hand.
Fa la la la la la la la la la.

I lost my head for a peerless hour
Hunted hind harried in the gloom
And my True Thomas in the tower.
Fa la la la la la la la la la.

Six headless horses to lead me home;
Hunted hind harried in the gloom
A headless coachman; a hollow crown.
Fa la la la la la la la la la.

Blickling Hall and grounds.

13. The Ballad of Anne Boleyn and The Burglar[7]

I stole to the door of Blickling Hall
On the nineteenth night of a moonlit May
And met the ghost of Anne Boleyn
Shining bright as day.

Six headless horses drew her coach
A haunted headless coachman drove,
'Give them their head!' she laughed, then turned
On me her look of love.

'I lost my hart in the darkest chase,
On the dying fall of a hunting horn.
I lost my head for the rose of the world
And the rose withered on the thorn.

'A death-white moon with a raven head
And a smile like a blossom of lovely May
I sold my heart for a worldly crown
And I'll take your breath away.'

'I'm not your True Thomas!' I cried in dread
And her witch head turned in its rotting shroud
'Ah! You've named the angel who guards my grave,'
And she hid her moon face in a cloud.

'I lost your hart in the darkest chase
On the dying fall of a hunting horn.
I lost my head for the rose of the world
And the rose withered on the thorn.

Julie Morrissey

---

[7] For an extra *frisson*, this ballad may be to sung to Henry VIII's own tune 'Greensleeves'

Vanessa Wood-Davies

14. The Ballad Of Edmund Wood
(The Strange Death of Catholic England)
for Aude

"various sums for repairs to the city wall and the Fyeing (cleaning) of the river, and £10 to repair the road between Norwich and Attleborough…20 Shillings apiece to 20 poore maydens for their marriage… £20 to poore men's children within Norwich to be brought up to lernynge…."

The Will of Edmund Wood, Mayor of Norwich and creator of Fye Bridge House (d. 1548)

Go steady stairwise as you come and go, Sir.
I lived here once; I am the ghost of Wood
- County Sheriff Alderman Edmund Wood -
A big-framed, sturdy, rich-grained merchant grocer
As solid and as warm as you could know, Sir,
With roots in river trade and limbs that stood
Through Henry's heady scythings and made good,
A Mayor of Norwich, but not lofty, No, Sir!

For Edmund's goods sail up the river, his goods sail down
And wholesome business there is done and nourishes the town.

What noble feet, I wonder, trod this Hall
When smoke could not escape from fires below
Except to drift from high hole or from window?
What blessedness a chimney brings to all!
Who cares to live in parlours like the noble,
And keep their Hall for entrance, feasts and show?
I build my nest above but, in a glow,
Stand grounded at my fireplace when you call.

For Edmund's goods sail up the river, his goods sail down
And wholesome business there is done and nourishes the town.

I've made a tidy pile so why not build one?
And as St Clement's is my place on earth,
My hive of city labour, my life's work,
Let Sexton's Manor, Aylsham, be my heaven;
It tickles me to build and run a mansion

42

Like those whose fortune comes to them by birth;
Though mine has come by labour, it is worth
More love for that, love arduously won.

For Edmund's goods sail up the river, his goods sail down
And wholesome business there is done and nourishes the town.

Some say my open-handedness was taint,
My last benevolence a sharp desire
To buy my soul from purgatorial fire;
That we rich men of Catholic times would fain
Give poor men twenty pounds for higher gain
With Mary Queen of Heaven and aspire
Repairing river, wall or road to hire her;
By aiding maids and scholars, buy a saint.

For Edmund's goods sail up the river, his goods sail down
And wholesome business there is done and nourishes the town.

But heaven is the treasure we have given
To brides and scholars ... or to Fye the river,
For city wall ... or road to Attleborough -
An upstairs floor in air, or else a dungeon
In God the Father's house, my life the mansion
Of rooms I earned from widow, woodman, weaver
(And Flemish Maddermarket-stinking dye and lucre!)
And joined as one, on earth as here in heaven.

For Edmund's goods sail up the river, his goods sail down
And wholesome business there is done and nourishes the town.

For man must eat as well as bow and flatter
And cities grow from traffic, purse and labour
Since all is founded there, or else on sand;
Though nobled by my country house and land
(A family crest remains to clinch the matter)
My island's one in substance with my neighbour.

And the river laughs softly under summer leaves
And the ghost of Catholic England floats away to the seas.

15. The Ballad of Kett's Rebellion[8] (1549)

"This Memorial was placed here by the citizens of Norwich in reparation and honour to a notable and courageous leader in the long struggle of the common people of England to escape from a servile life into the freedom of just conditions."
Plaque on the wall of Norwich Castle

As I lay down on Mousehold Heath,
I heard two corbies beak to beak,
'It's cold as death, fifteen below.
To Norwich Castle let us go.

'Upon its wall, a traitor hangs
Who led last summer's rebel gangs:
Twelve thousand men, a city strong,
Unfencing nine and twenty wrongs.'

The Commons' land, he gave it back
Then led their time-honoured attack
And his bare bones shall be his plaque
Till crows are white and snows are black.

At Dussindale they broke his army;
His brother hanged on Wymondham Abbey;
His name is blood in church and state,
We'll pick his bones to celebrate.

His brave old England: shabby crops
Outselling woollens in the shops;
The oak its heart until its bark
Is cut to build a new car park.'

The Commons' land, he gave it back
Then led their time-honoured attack
And his bare bones shall be his plaque
Till crows are white and snows are black.

---

[8] Yeoman Farmer Robert Kett's 29 demands sought to limit the power of a gentry turbo-charged by Henry VIII's social revolution; keep them out of village life; put a brake on runaway economic change, protect common land and rights, and remind the clergy of their vocation.

'His brave new England on the hill
In narrow streets and arms fulfilled;
Its oak near Hethersett will stand
While people matter more than plans.'

The Commons' land, he gave it back
Then led their time-honoured attack
And his bare bones shall be his plaque
Till crows are white and snows are black.[9]

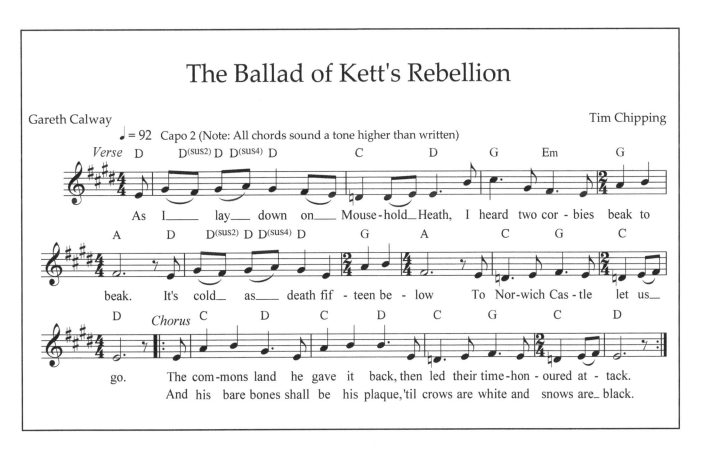

9   'The Twa Corbies' (pessimistic) and 'The Three Ravens' (optimistic) show how differently the same tale of a dead knight can grow in different soils. Both moods are reflected in this homage to those ballads and to that knight of the commons Robert Kett. While one ancient oak associated with him was summarily cut down for a city centre carpark, the other has been preserved in his honour.

16. The Ballad of Cromwell's Head

"And indeed, being in the heat of battle, I forbade them to spare any that were in arms in the town... and truly I believe this bitterness will save much blood through the goodness of God"

Cromwell: Letter from Drogheda, 1649

A headless horseman dropped his head
And dropped his grin as well
Says I to the horsehead, why the long face?
Says he, 'I've come from hell.

Though I stained the Pale from green to red,
In Sixteen Forty Nine,
Grave robbers butcher my body and head
For an English capital crime.

I chopped off the head of a tyrannous king
And a traitor to his land
Forged an English Republican Army
With Bible and sword in hand.

O, they dig up my body, chop off my head,
And spike it on Westminster Hall
Not for my high over-righteous zeal
But for my Republican gall.'

'Cut off his head with the cown upon it,
God damn this King!' I cried,
'Only tyrants will tremble, recalling this day,
Good men recall it with pride.'

The King sold his soul to the Bloody Maries,
The old foe, his fingers crossed:
'Better the Irish you know how to cheat
Than the Roundhead who can't be bossed.'

The only decade of English history
With the English at its head
But Good King Charles's fairy-tory
Is anything but dead.

O, they dig up my body, chop off my head,
And spike it on Westminster Hall
Not for my high over-righteous zeal
But for my Republican gall.'

I Scotched their alliance of haggled souls
With a miracle at Dunbar
And the Britain I ruled with a sword of steel
Was gentler-bridled by far

And I drowned your father's town in blood
When green was the wasted colour,
Of Catholic wiping out Catholic in arms
And brother reducing brother.

The greatest England for four hundred years
And its meanest act in Drogheda
I sent native Irish to Connacht or hell,
But they send me to hell for the other.

O, they dig up my body, chop off my head,
And spike it on Westminster Hall
Not for my high over-righteous zeal
But for my Republican gall.'

17. The Ballad of Freeborn John

The bloodiest war in our history
And one in four of us died
For a castled king on a stagnant throne
In a revolutionary tide.

'I spilt my blood so I need a voice!'
Cries Freeborn John at Putney,
'Who dies for England is England's king,
We are no grandee's army.

'The poorest man in England has
The right to live as the greatest,
Our God's the All in all, our king's
The Christ in every breast.'

The bloodiest war in our history
And one in four of us died
For a castled king on a stagnant throne
In a revolutionary tide.

We're the voice of the Freeborn Englishman
That was raised at Magna Carta,
The Dissenting flag of the Good Old Cause,
The common or garden martyr.

I rose with Tyler, Straw and Ball
When peasants shook the kingdom,
I was sold down that river of blood by a king
Who hawked the soul of England.

We need no manor house and land
To fix our permanent interest,
We fight for England, our rights and ourselves:
No mercenary business.

The bloodiest war in our history
And one in four of us died
For a castled king on a stagnant throne
In a revolutionary tide.

48

I will rise at Kett's Hill and Tolpuddle,
I will fall at Peterloo,
March to Chartist hell and a Newport hotel
To win this Britain for you,

Die a million deaths in two world wars
Though the portion's not so many
As died for Charles, that Man of Blood,
And in our redcoat Army.

A new model England truly advanced,
Through rank and royal sin
In a cavalry charge to a Future Now
Whose 'God Not Man Is King'.[10]

The bloodiest war in our history
And one in four of us died
For a castled king on a stagnant throne
In a revolutionary tide.

10   Cromwell's republican epitaph. Charles Stuart lost a Civil War most imagined would be settled by sieges &
      mediaeval castles; Cromwell won with it with modern cavalry charges and a new model infantry.

18. The Ballad of The Backwoods Cavalier

Hamon L'Estrange of Hunstanton Hall (was) a sexagenarian Cavalier living in the grand style with expensive tastes; expensive sons running up debts; eighteen servants (including a falconer and a fool) and a black marble floor in his stables. ...He... led a Town Hall coup, declaring himself, on 13 August – without any mandate whatsoever - 'governor of Lynn for the king'. The borough's two MPs, John Percival and Thomas Toll, were put under house arrest.

Hamon's youngest son Roger, after fighting at his father's (losing) side at the Siege of Lynn, joined the King at Oxford. He was 'an enthusiastic, hot-headed, plausible young man... perpetually evolving ambitious schemes and failing to bring them to fruition.' He convinced the King, against all the evidence, that a spirit of Royalist resistance remained at Lynn and that he was the man to lead it.' The King supplied him with a commission and a letter, dated November 1644, promising him 'a considerable power' to consolidate the uprising. Roger went straight to Appleton Hall, owned by the Royalist William Paston of Oxnead, and enlisted a Lynn sea captain named Leaman in his hare-brained scheme, who promptly shopped him to the authorities in Lynn.

Magazine Cottage, Sedgeford, is believed to have been a powder magazine built in 1640 by Hamon L'Estrange, Lord of the Manor of Sedgeford.

My father leapt upon his high horse
And galloped it hard into Lynn,
"I seize this Parliamentary town,
Declare it for the King!"

"You have no mandate!" cried Mayor and MPs
Laughed Dad, "Arrest those knaves!
Cavalier bravado has come to town
Which you from yourselves I'll save."

Though Cromwell's preachies at the Gate
Of Lynn as at Heaven knock,
Our stained glass windows shoot all to hell,
Our royal passage block,

My dad's the lord of this manor, say I,
And magazine farmers are we,
Against the odds and facts and slings
Of cowherd reality.

Say I "Great king, your royal East
And loyal Lynn, I'll re-seize 'em,

They're rebels for Your Majesty
And I'm the man to lead 'em!"

The king he writes a broad letter
And thrusts it into my hand,
"Roger L'Estrange shall rule in Lynn
With phantoms I command."

We live and die a chevalier's life,
Have it all and spend even more
On a falconer, fool, on a fowl-mouthed fop's
Black marble stable floor.

My dad's the lord of this manor, say I,
And magazine farmers are we,
Against the odds and facts and slings
Of cowherd reality.

From Oxford Town to Norfolk woods
The four winds see me ride
And show my fine letter to a Jack
His poor coat to turn or bribe.

'Captain Leaman' is that seaman,
Cries he, 'Er, we'll talk anon,
I must now to Lynn awhile but will
Return here to Appleton."

He rides to Colonel Walton and brings
Six redcoats in disguise,
"Show us His Royal Traitor's hand!'
They pinch me as a spy.

My dad's the lord of this manor, say I,
And magazine farmers are we,
Against the odds and facts and slings
Of cowherd reality.

19. The Ballad of the Cod Fishers

Homage to an unsung and underpaid group of East Anglian heroes who, when England's population was booming at a time of unprecedented economic growth between the end of the Elizabethan period and the Industrial Revolution, sailed north through hell and high water to the Arctic circle and brought back the cheap nutritious foodstuff a growing nation needed. And precious little thanks they had for it.

The Mayor he sits in Norwich town
Eating his snow-white cod
'This fair meat of the northern wastes
Is English as our God.

We need a fleet to bring it home
To feed our growing nation
Of salts who sail close to the wind
And closer to starvation.'

The frozen price of Iceland cod
Is Norwich Market cheap
But the rising tax on catch and salt
Makes tar and fishwife weep.

Oh these chippy men of Nelson's breed
Who braved the northern seas
They paid the highest price of all
And the meanest price received.

The Iceland fleet sails north in March,
Great ships of forty men,
The doughtiest hearts in England's shores
From Eastern shire and fen.

Such crews as drive the men of war
To English Victory
Cured by these waves, the saltest men
Who ever put to sea.

Fierce winds and tides have blocked for weeks
Their course through Pentland Firth,
The nearest place to death and hell
On all God's Christian earth.

Chorus

And the Danish King sits like a storm
That broods upon a shore:
'Six miles off Iceland you must toss
Nor trade nor fish there more!'

'No time, sea-lads, for those native cures
And cods hung out to dry,
Our summer catch is steeped in salt
To keep it from the fly

And salt is taxed at rising rates
By Oliver's excise
And ten score cod per loaded ship
His officers will prise.'

Chorus

Widows and traders who keep afloat
These ventures seal their loan
With a premium more than twice the mean
For so many come not home.

O long the Jack Tar's journey home
And deep the briny ocean
And toothsome was the bone-white cod
That fed a hungry nation.

And long the Norfolk[11] fishwives stand
With wood combs in their hair
In August at the water's edge
When fish nor men appear.
Chorus

---

[11]   King's Lynn, Yarmouth and Wells-next-the-Sea were all major cod fishing ports.

The Ballad of the Cod Fishers

Gareth Calway

Tim Chipping

Have you tried it yet?

20. The Ballad of Sir Robert Walpole (Bob of Lynn)

Knight of the slightly drooping Garter,
King of Bankrupt Hall,
Lord of the Backstairs Tower Tryst,
Stout Adam of the Fall.

Richeldis, Julian, Sawtrey, Nelson,
Boleyn and Boudicca tall,
Margery, Fanny, Turnip, Kett,
Old Tom Paine and all.

Norfolk and good our heroes stand
With something pure about 'em
But none more Norfolk nor more good
Than Dodgy Bob of Houghton.

Sir Robert Walpole, King of Sink,
The Pharaoh of the Flaw,
The not so bumpkin Norfolk dumplin'
Loophole in the Law.

The first Prime Minister and still
Unequalled in that office;
The backwoods front-man, laughing loud,
The Prince of Peace – and Profits.

The Age he named is hero-free,
No children need to know.
They keep it off the syllabus,
No killers boldly go.

No Bonnie Charlie anthems, saints,
No bagpipe calls to arms;
Just German Georges 1 and 2,
Enlightenment and farms.

The beau, the rake, the dandy, fop,
The mistress-paying knights,
The hypocrite with itchy palm:
'All *these* men have their price.'

Sir Robert Walpole, Count of Cash,
The Pharaoh of the Flaw,

The not so bumpkin country speakin'
Loophole in the Law.

His Babel built 'too far from London'[12]
Under a Norfolk bushel
The Neptune and Britannia Rampant
Counting House as Castle.

His bust and Caesar hairdo placed
A British cut above
The classic Mantle he assumed
Of Wisdom, Justice, Love.

Removed the timber duty while
He ordered his supplies,
Avoided Finished Buildings tax
With one unfinished frieze.

Sir Robert Walpole, Earl of Ease,
The Pharaoh of the Flaw,
The ruddy cunnin' Norfolk rulin'
Loophole in the Law.

Our burly boisterous backhand Bob
Was bawdy in his cups
Had heart-to-hearts with kings and queens
Yet kept the common touch.

And when the South Sea Bubble burst
And drowned both Whig and Tory,
He saved the country with a speech
And rode the tide to glory

Avoided War for eighteen years
Of Profit weighed with cost,
'They ring the bells, they'll wring their hands,'
He said when Peace was lost.

Sir Robert Loophole, Laughin' Bob,
The Prophet of the Flaw,
Three hundredweight of Killed Cock Robin[13]
Loophole in the Law.

---

12   The Duke of Wellington's response when offered Houghton Hall as a palatial gift from the nation after Waterloo. Instead, it stood empty throughout the Victorian period.

13   Walpole really was this weight (23 stone) by the time he died and took some burying in the parish church of his home estate at Houghton. The nursery rhyme 'Who Killed Cock Robin?' was first printed at the time of Walpole's fall in 1742 and contains multiple references to it.

21. The Ballad of the Brown Lady

Dorothy Townshend née Walpole was wife of Foreign Secretary 'Turnip' Townshend of Raynham and sister of Sir Robert Walpole of Houghton, Britain's first PM. Walpole famously observed that Townsend was happy when 'the family firm was Townsend and Walpole' but much less so when it became 'Walpole and Townsend'. Dorothy died on March 29 1726 (under George I) but was famously photographed haunting the staircase at Raynham Hall on September 19 1936 (during the brief, dubiously affiliated and abdicated reign of Edward VIII.)

Brown Lady of the Haunted Halls
Where root and pig are rife
They say he killed her in his wrath
Who loved her more than life.

'Where eyes should be, dark hollows were,'
Said one bold guest at Raynham
Another shot her shadow as she
Disappeared behind them.

What I have seen, I pray to God,
I'll not again, *Geist outen!'*
Cried George IV 'I will not sleep
Another hour at Houghton!

She died the queen of Norfolk's reign,
First Lady of the Whigs,
They took her photo on the stairs
In 1936. (Ah!)

She loved her Viscount Charlie true,
She loved her brother Robin,
She was the heart that joined them when
The family firm was thriving.

And now she spooks the titled dogs
That guard the beds at night
And gives her guests in Halls, on stairs
And blackout roads a fright.

For love's the witch to rule them all
Who more than turnips love
What are we else but rutting swine?
She answers from above:

I was the queen of Norfolk's reign,
First Lady of the Whigs,
I am the Ghost of England Past,
The Circe of her pigs. (Ah!)

22. The Ballad of Turnip Townshend

"Whoever can make two ears of corn or two blades of grass grow upon a spot of ground where only one grew before, would deserve better of mankind and do more essential service to his country than the whole race of politicians put together." Swift

He took the job that couldn't be done.
By God, he couldn't do it!
He ploughed against his inner grain
And stuck his foot right through it.

His fits of spleen were legendary,
He brooked no contradictions,
A bladed feather-spitting lord,
'A slave to brutal passions.'

'Perplexed and slow in argument,
Inelegant in language',
They sent him to the House of Lords;
He spoke like Wurzel Gummidge.

The voice of Norfolk at the court,
Its Lord Lieutenant he;
He died of apoplexy but
He lives in every tree.

He makes the world go round and bucks
His pheasant-pluckers' earnships;
He turns the Earth in cultured hand:
He's wonderful with turnips.

As Foreign Secretary he schemed
Though briefed to keep the peace
Alliances against our friends
And with our enemies.

A diplomat who spurned to spin
A web of subterfuge,
He told it bluntly as it was,
Offensively and huge.

When Walpole, brother to his wife
Presumed to doubt his words,
He collared his old *bon ami*
And both went for their swords.

'Robbing Bob!' 'You Charlie, Sir!
And haughty in your carriage!'
'Who'll kill Cock Robin?' 'I, Sir, I!'
'Beshrew your dead wife's marriage!'

He turns his back upon the world
And bucks his peasants' earnships;
He turns the Earth in cultured hand:
He's wonderful with turnips.

He led the Revolution
From a rich man's high estate
Made model farming *a la mode*,
Enlightened stall and gate.

He made a science of the sod,
An Athens of the yard,
Went Dutch with clover and *sainfoin*,
He barned and hedged and marled.

He showed the world his meat and veg,
His four rotation art
And made a well-bred vanguard of
The Norfolk farmer's cart.

"What ought not, cannot, be allowed,
What makes my choler churn, it's
What small proportion of your farm,
Stout yeoman, is in turnips!"

He makes the world go round and bucks
His pheasant-pluckers' earnships;
He turns the Earth in cultured hand:
He's wonderful with turnips.

23. The Ballad of Fanny Burney
For Alison

There must be some magic in the water at Lynn – the Celts certainly thought so – the port is plausibly the fount of three literary genres. A 'tradition that lingers' places Chaucer the Father of English Poetry's birthplace here; Lynn's Margery Kempe wrote the first English autobiography and Jane Austen herself hailed Lynn's Frances Burney – particularly her Cecilia and Camilla - as paving the way for the 'Austen' novel.

'I offered some few words in favour of my poor abused town the land of my nativity - of the world's happiness – we discoursed a little time and Hetty suddenly cried out 'Hush hush, Mama's in the next room. If she hears us we two will be whipt. And Fanny will have a sugar plumb' 'Aye cried Maria tis her defending Lynn which makes Mama (Fanny's stepmother, Mrs Allen, Lynn born and bred) so fond.' **Fanny Burney's diary**

'Your shyness and slyness and pretending to know nothing never took me in whatever you may do with others. I always knew you for a toadling.' **Dr Johnson**

> Of Halls and harpies, harpsichords,
> Society and Sin,
> She wrote her sugar-plumbing words,
> Sweet Fanny B of Lynn.
>
> Up-laddering Queen Charlotte's robes
> And blood-Blue Stocking works,
> The glittering Balls of Johnsons, Garricks,
> Montagus and Burkes.
>
> The snake, the cad, the ingénue,
> Bad-manners and bad hearts,
> She clocked them with a lady lash,
> A tongue to make them smart.
>
> The tale that stings, but draws the sting,
> The venom-purging venom,
> The Berkshire Hunts and toady Halls,
> The coiling steps to heaven.
>
> *The latest in the Linnet line*
> *Of Liter-artery*
> *Like Geoff and Marge she wrote the Book*
> *And laid a dynasty.*

Warwick Jones (right) with Waterline

The King run mad at royal Kew,
The understated feeling,
The cutting through the gothic vein,
The blood across the ceiling.

Her lovely Eves with rolling eyes
And lady shakers' wit
All sliding down the horny snakes,
The matron's hissy fit,

To rise at last through tested mind
And heart's adversity
To spirited degrees of Love in
Swoonaversity

While their creator suffered tea
With gossip and coquette,
In smalling talk and paralysing
Social etiquette,

The latest in the Linnet line
Of Liter-artery
Like Lollard Will she wrote the Book
And laid a dynasty.

The fathead Norwich bishop stumped
By her more worthy kneeling,
The brain as sharp as steel, the breast
As cleanly feeling

The day they told her - needlessly -
'Madame, do *not* restrain
The twenty minute scream, the in-
Describable pain,

From vicarage garden cabin maid
To Madame Guillotine
And that Napoleonic blade,
She stayed awake and keen.

Her soul in irony survived
The caught romantic breath
Where Shelley's gothic monster cry
Ran out of death.

The latest in the Linnet line
Of Liter-artery
Like Geoff and Marge she wrote the Book
And laid a dynasty.

The Burneys

The Ballad of Fanny Burney

Vanessa Wood-Davies

24. Just Like Tom Paine's Blues

Midsummer nightmare driving
The roads around Tom Paine,
The June moon had me crying
Were all his dreams in vain?

The woods were blurred with menace,
I could not read the signs,
My Common Sense was fading,
It has so many times.

The Rights of Man and Woman
Like road-kill on the track,
Too deep and late the forest
To think of turning back.

Midsummer in the greenwood,
Midwinter chill within,
The starry sky of reason,
The night as dark as sin.

They made a film in Thetford,
A set of posing thieves
Who aped Tom's generation
To lies and mock-believe.

The Age of Revolution
They turned to smoke and lust,
His California dreaming
To boom and boob and bust.

This Burke who rolls the camera
Who never made a Scene:
America, the Human:
Our common State and dream.

Midsummer in the greenwood,
Midwinter chill within,
The starry sky of reason,
The night as dark as sin.

At midnight, I'm still wearing
King George's darkened shades
My part's short-sighted vision:
I tear it from my face.

Tom Paine is pointing down the road
To new world Washington;
I meet the clear and steady eye
Of Revolution

That maps a Constitution through
The dead decaying mess,
The Royal Burkshire Hunters' praise
Of murky wilderness.

Midsummer in the greenwood,
I see it clearly now,
The angel moon of reason,
The Man of Thetford's brow.[14]

---

[14] I'd been acting the part of Burke in a film about Paine made in Thetford. I used short distance specs as my method of playing Burke's limited vision. One actor took an entire evening and nineteen takes to remember his lines and I was so exhausted driving home through the midsummer midnight forest, I thought my eyes had packed up – I had to get out of the car to read the road signs. Ten miles south of King's Lynn, I realised I was still wearing my character's specs. I use all this as a metaphor for Tom Paine's optimistic revolutionary clarity ('The Rights Of Man') seeing through the obfuscating King Georgian gloom beautified by Edmund Burke ('Reflections on the French Revolution'). The UEA student who spray-painted BURKE on a wall in 1976 about his history lecturer couldn't possibly comment.

Just like Tom Paine's Blues

Gareth Calway   Tim Chipping

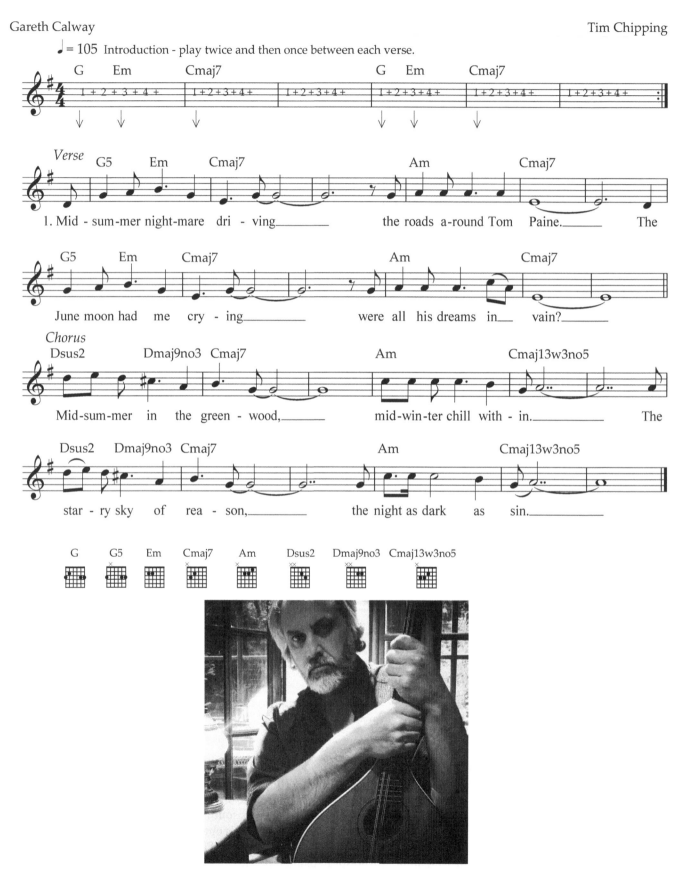

Tim Chipping.

25. Half God, Half Nelson

"Norfolk volunteers- worth two of other men ..." (Captain Nelson, 1793)

Our Admiral's head it has one eye
Heave away! Heave away!
His empty sleeve's the flag we fly.
'Tell my wife I'm killed,' we say.

Heave away Horatio's boys
Heave away! Heave away!
Heave away and make a Victory noise
From Burnham to Trafalgar.

He hunted polar bears, the lad
Heave away! Heave away!
'To fetch a white rug to my dad.'
'Tell my wife I'm killed,' we say.

Chorus

Mosquitoes bit him half to death:
Heave away! Heave away!
'I'll die a hero's life instead'
'Tell my wife I'm killed,' we say.

Chorus

Off Corsica, his eye foresworn,
Heave away! Heave away!
'I got a little hurt this morn.'
'Tell my wife I'm killed,' we say.

Chorus

Off Cape St Vincent, breaking ranks,
Heave away! Heave away!
He won the day and England's thanks.
'Tell my wife I'm killed,' we say.

Chorus

Our king's right hand at Santa Cruz;
Heave away! Heave away!
A night to seize; an arm to lose.
'Tell my wife I'm killed,' we say.

Chorus

'A peerage or Westminster crypt!'
Heave away! Heave away!
He sinks the French from here to Egypt
'Tell my wife I'm killed,' we say.

Chorus

'You'll discontinue!' flagged his Admiral.
Heave away! Heave away!
'My blind eye does not see your signal!'
'Tell my wife I'm killed,' we say.

Chorus

'Redoubtable' sharpshooters spy him
Heave away! Heave away!
'They've done for me at last. I'm dying.'
'Tell my wife I'm killed,' we say.

Chorus

26. The Ballad of the Ruined Hall [15]

Strange that an Encyclopaedic Age
Leaves Fye Bridge House un-reckoned on its page.
But wait! a lace-cuffed bard with limpid eye
Is halted by a spirit thrilling by...

'I haunt the former greatness of this Hall -
Before a ceiling floored its gothic stage,
My cheek is paper-white, my poppy
Mouth the blemish on a poet's page.'

'Consumptive spirit! Wild! Unbounded! Free!
O sleepless beauty past all human measure.'
She falls upon the thorns of life. I bleed!
Her gates of Eden open at my ple-....

'I pine for Ruined Hall and sing
An elegy of days before a floor
Plucked window's eye and clipped the wings
Of church-like space, staired flights unknown before!'

I charge her cup again, again, and ever:
Our Road to Wisdom's Palace is Excess;
Her blood lips wailing for her demon lover
And black eyes staring from her naked breasts!'

Repeat 'Consumptive spirit...' Chorus

Alas! A pounding at the door, the vision flies.
The Parson calls on business, and the Poem ...dies!

---

[15]   Fye Bridge House, Norwich, in the Romantic Era.

Doin Different raising Julian in their Heaven and Hell show at the Bicycle Shop, Norwich.

27. The Ballad of Bread or Blood (1816)

"I might as well be hanged as starved" (Richard Rutter, a rioter at Ely)

"When the rich plunder the poor of their rights, it becomes an example to the poor to plunder the rich of their property." (Tom Paine)

It was 'the year without a summer',
The price of bread was sky-high;
The Poor Law kept our wages low;
The farmers watched us die.

The Iron Duke called us heroes,
The 'Victors of Waterloo',
We came home to our starving children
With no work for victors to do.

'8 shillings, Sir, to work all week,
Two pounds of bread for to buy,
To till the England we fought to save,
To be maimed for, to kill for, to die.'

'What do you want?' they ask us,
The Judges and Kings of the age.
'Our children are starving – to feed them!
Give us a living wage!

Our bit of land too dear to fence,
We sold to the enclosers;
Now we fence-ditch-hedge it for the squire
As landless labourers.

Aye, enclosure robs the common rights
We had, it ploughs the grass
Whereon we fed the cow we've lost,
The horse, the pig, the ass.

I joined the Army then to feed
My bleak-eyed family
But the war just parted rich from poor,
Made wealth my enemy.

'What do you want?' they ask us,
The Judges and Kings of the age.
'Our children are starving – to feed them!
Give us a living wage!

"Your riot is for riot's sake!"
Those JPs say, their station
To balance farmers, millers, shops
With waged men, as a nation.

On the old world of noblesse oblige
'All help themselves' is carved
They to our rights, we to their wealth,
He hangs as well who starves!

Machines steal my work, agues my house,
High prices my wages low,
From vicious Fenland damp and floods,
To pub and to riot we go!   (a horn sounds)

'What do you want?' they ask us,
The Judges and Kings of the age.
'Our children are starving – to feed them!
Give us a living wage!'

Andy Wall

The Ballad of Bread or Blood (1816)

Gareth Calway

Andy Wall

It was 'the year with-out a sum-mer',the price of bread was sky high;____ The
Poor Law kept our__ wa-ges low; The__ far-mers watched us die.____ The
Iron Duke called us her-oes, The 'Vic-tors of Wa-ter-loo',____ We
came home to our__ star-ving chil-dren With no work for vic-tors to do.____ "Eight
shil-lings, Sir, to work all week, Two pounds of bread for to buy,____ To
till the Eng-land we fought to save, to be maimed for, to kill for, to die.
"What do you want?" they ask us,____ The jud-ges and Kings of the age.____ "Our
chil-dren are star-ving to feed them!__ Give us a li-ving wage!"_
Our bit of land too dear to fence, we sold to the en-clo-sers; Now we
fence-ditch-hedge it__ for__ the squire As__ land-less la-bour-ers.____ Aye, en-
-clo-sure robs the com-mon rights We had, it ploughs the grass Where-

-on we fed the cow we've lost, The horse, the pig, the ass. I

joined the ar-my then to feed My bleak-eyed fa-mi-ly; But the

war just par-ted rich from poor; Made wealth my e-ne-my.

"What do you want?" they ask us, The jud-ges and Kings of the age. "Our

chil-dren are star-ving to feed them! Give us a li-ving wage!

"Your ri-ot is for ri-ot's sake!" Those J Ps say, their sta-tion To

ba-lance far-mers, mil-lers, shops with waged men, as a na-tion. On the

old world of no-blesse ob-lige 'All help them-selves' is carved, They

to our rights, we to their wealth, He hangs as well who starves! Ma-chines

steal my work, a-gues my house, High pri-ces my wa-ges low, From

vi-cious Fen-land damp and floods, To pub and ri-ot we go!

"What do you want?" they ask us, The jud-ges and Kings of the age. "Our

chil-dren are star-ving to feed them! Give us a li-ving wage!

77

28. The Ballad of Elizabeth Fry

(b.1780, daughter of John Gurney of Earlham Hall, a Norwich banker and Quaker; married London Quaker Joseph Fry in 1800; formed the Association for the Improvement of Female Prisoners in Newgate there in 1817; helped persuade Peel's government to reform the penal code in 1822, including conditions of transportation; in old age forced herself to petition Prince Albert and, in 1842, addressed a Quaker meeting out of apparent madness, in a wheelchair, ending with Isaiah's *'Thine eyes shall see the king in his beauty: they shall behold the land that is very far off'*; d. Oct 12 1845)

The quality streets of the 'Nineties,
Toy soldiers on painted tins
With chocolate-box ladies in dresses
And French Revolution within.

I'm a Gurney of Earlham Hall, Norwich,
The Cathedral City is mine
With its ladies and literati,
And Prince William to dance and to dine.

In my riding-high scarlet habit,
I shyly join the dance,
Setting my feathered cap at the troops
Bound for Napoleon's France.

These Quaker meetings, must I go?
I'm ill, give my excuses.
Love God but loathe hysterics, cant.
I don't know what God's use is.

'I must not flirt, be tetchy, proud,
Be vain, the children's scold,
Be pretty, tall and passionate,
Be seventeen years old.'

One Quaker-silent day, Love's star
Hoves like the Sun before me,
The distant God I guessed, I *see,*
I'm weeping but I'm happy.

God's nightmares come, I'm all at sea;
The tide flows in and takes me,
'Elizabeth' is washed away,
Her drowning breath forsakes me.

These Quaker meetings, must I go?
I'm ill, give my excuses.
Love God but loathe hysterics, cant.
I don't know what God's use is.

White-robed, I brave the staring streets
Serve poor and falsely damned,
The press-ganged man whose wife with babe
Was starved so stole then hanged;

Barred slimy dungeons swarmed with rats,
Cruel chains and iron collars,
Beasted gaolbirds, brutal guards,
Half-naked nights of horrors;

The wagon loads brought to the docks
Like cows for transportation
To lives of crime – no other work
"You can't reform a felon!"

These Quaker meetings, must I go?
I'm ill, give my excuses.
Love God but loathe hysterics, cant.
I don't know what God's use is.

She didn't rant against the Law,
False judges, gaolers, prisons,
She touched the inmates' desperate hearts,
Cared for their ill-starred children,

She taught them, got them work for bread;
Brought faith and self-respect
To filth, disorder, chaos, noise:
The gaolbirds did the rest.

Her act of faith – let Newgate be
A place to be reformed,
Not punished, demonised, disowned;
The State observed and learned.

These Quaker meetings, must I go?
I have no more excuses.
Love God and loathe hysterics, can
And do know what God's use is.

29. The Ballad of Susan Nobes

"The evening (July 5, 1819, in the pretty Norfolk village of Sedgeford) *was most beautiful. The birds sang sweetly. People were busy working in the fields, men and women with hooks around bundles and sheaves of corn and all was peace and quietness... The schoolmistress saw Susan Nobes remarkably active and happy."* Eliza Cunningham A Narrative of Facts. (British Library)

'Come out in the dark lane, lonely boy,
Leave your laptop and play with me.
Leave your father and mother and holiday home
For my wildwood and wicked sea.'

A gone-tomorrow full-moon face
In bonnet and Sunday best;
A goose ran up and down my flesh,
My hair stood like a crest.

'I'd die to hold a girl like you,
So fashion-hungry thin
But fear there is no heart behind
That sly come-hither grin.

'There's maggots in your Sunday best,
Your bony heroin chic's
A shade too grave about your mouth,
Your vulture-grinning beak.'

'I've been Death's bride two hundred years
And much too young to die,
Let me take you back to 1819,
The Fifth Day of July.'

The Squire rode down my father's door
'All hands to the pump!' honked he.
'Sir, I'm weary from working your bone-dry fields,
'My family hath need of me!'

'You're weary from working my golden fields
But my House expects a neighbour
And my Stream has dried in the lower field
And my Pump demands your labour.'

Our childish shrieks filled the heaven-blue
Played hide and seek round the paves
Laughed under the leaves of Eden-green
And kiss-chased through the graves.

The tardy teacher loomed at the gate,
Seized my pretty lobes,
Snatched my posy of burial flowers
'You're a hell child, Susan Nobes!'

The sunlit schoolroom candle burned
A flame that barely lightened;
A stroke before the clock struck nine
It devilishly brightened.

A growl and rumble at the door,
As dark as pitch in the room,
A sizzling hiss, like a snake on the roof,
An ear-exploding boom.

'Prayer,' scorned the teacher, 'is stronger than rain!'
The dark began to splinter
In lightning tongues as bright as noon,
It grew as cold as winter.

'God save us!' screamed the children all,
The teacher tore her gown,
The rain came down in ice and hail,
The sky tipped upside down.

A stained glass window-angel smashed,
I kneeled and tried to pray,
A fiery crack of sulphur took
My girlish breath away.

The flickering lightning licked the tower,
Scorched a yard-wide hole in the wall
And from where my Saviour hung on high
Great blocks began to fall.

'O Robert, our Susan's lost in the storm.
What kept you away so long?'
'The Squire needed water, he got his wish,
But where is our daughter gone?'

'I sent her to Sunday School, oh Robert,
And I fear my choice was cursed.
For none alive has seen such a Flood
Of gravesoil in the church.

He forged the cross under baked Dove Hill,
Its Wash rolled like a tide,
He climbed over hill to the rain-drenched crowd
And took the teacher aside.

'Where's Susan?' he asked, as quiet as Death,
'I believe she is with her Saviour.'
'You left her alone in the schoolroom and fled?'
His question got no answer.

He waded the Flood and past the font
At which he'd named his daughter;
A schoolroom chill as any tomb
Awash with blocks and mortar.

He found me lifeless upon the floor,
My temples charred with flame,
He clenched me in his arms and wept
A tide he'll never stem.

'Come out in the dark lane, lonely boy,
Leave your laptop and play with me.
Leave your father and mother and holiday home
For my wildwood and wicked sea.'

The Ballad of Susan Nobes

Vanessa Wood-Davies

30. The Ballad of Edith Cavell

... When Norfolk soldiers came to hide,
She joked of home and smiled
In accents shared, 'for Norfolk-men
I goo that extra mile.'

She sees the pale gold August wheat,
The oaken greens of home,
A mind's-eye Norfolk harvest wrapped
Around October's bones.

Six paces off, eight rifles point,
Death scarves her blue-grey eyes,
The woman stands and prays and waits
And still no shot arrives...

Her life is flashing by, the days
With Eddy on the beach
'When life was fresh and beautiful,
The country dear and sweet.'

'Love of country's not enough
And when they shoot me dead
Let bitterness and hatred die,'
Our Norfolk angel said.

... The clinic clean and welcoming
The poor and most forlorn;
A mother to her nurses clad
In angels' uniforms.

A spider crawled across the floor,
One screamed, would stamp it dead,
'A woman doesn't take a life,
She gives it,' Edith said.

The British held the line at Mons,
The French were in retreat,
All stranded men came to her door
Through Brussels' conquered streets.

'Love of country's not enough
And when they shoot me dead
Let bitterness and hatred die,'
Our Norfolk angel said.

One nurse too hot for German pride
They bullied as a spy,
Ede sent her home – with army secrets
Bandaged to her thigh!

La Libre Belgique was her text,
The Life of Christ her God;
Said Pinkhoff, Bergan, Mayer, Quien:
'Give her the firing squad.'

4 sneaks and spies to smoke her out,
3 days' interrogation.
She wouldn't lie…. They shot her dead
For love of more than nation.

'Love of country's not enough
And when they shoot me dead
Let bitterness and hatred die,'
Our Norfolk angel said.

31. The Ballad of Little Jimmy (The Vicar of Stiffkey)

"Harold Francis Davidson ('Little Jimmy') was loved by the villagers, who recognised his humanity and forgave him his transgressions. May he rest in peace." (epitaph in Stiffkey churchyard)

An actor cum rector,
His pulpit his stage,
Generous star of his parish's
Unlighted age.

Serves his country and king
In the First World War,
Comes home to a wife
Playing the whore.

Spends his weekdays in Soho
With poor girls undone,
25,000 fallen
On the streets of London.

Stiffkey to the Gate
Of the kirk and pearlies,
His trial grips the nation
By the short and curlies.

To the Stiffkey faithful
He's the open hand;
To the North Norfolk gentry
In the dock he stands.

RANDY RECTOR OF STIFFKEY's
The Fleet Street shtick;
Bishop Norwich calls in
A muck-raking Dick.

All the fallen absolve him
Save the one Dick decants
Down a bottle of lies
Even she recants.

Stiffkey to the Gate
Of the kirk and pearlies,
His trial grips the nation
By the short and curlies.

The Cathedral Inquisition
Meets to pre-Judge him,
The Snob-jobbing Old Boys
Defrock and degrade him.

He returns to the stage;
At Blackpool he rages,
Pleads his innocence, preaches
To lions in cages.

At Skeggy, he treads on
The big tail of Freddie
The Lion who shakes him
And leaves him for deadie.

The crowd cheers the show
But the show is over
For this Prostitutes' padre,
This Magdalene lover.

Stiffkey to the Gate
Of the kirk and pearlies,
His trial grips the nation
By the short and curlies.

32. The University of Esoteric Abbreviations (UEA)

Scar-smooth, this lady
Killer, savaged heart unseen
On the well-groomed sleeve.

Watch me dance, baby,
Watch me kick off these shoes,
These are the steps
I pretended to use.

Watch this hat, baby,
Over both eyes
Watch how it tips
A wink to the wise.

Watch this shirt, baby,
Torn to the heart,
This is how love
Strips us of art.

I've worn the pants, babe,
But love's split the crutch,
I really have nothing
But what you can touch.

Now you see, baby,
How do you react?
Now you see what's behind
My disappearing act?

A monastery built
Out of concrete abstractions
For courtly lovers,
This College of Young Ones,

With nights tolling in
Along vertigo walkways,
Freshers' Balls
And red-bedded maydays (*m'aidez*)

On his knight's velvet sleeve
The lady-killer's
Savaged heart unseen is
As crude as the miller's.

I've worn the armour,
L'amour's pierced the heart,
Unhorsed and outlanced
In a sensitive part.

Now you see, baby,
How do you react?
Now you see what's behind
My disappearing act?[16]

<hr>

[16]   I wrote this in my first term at UEA in 1975 about a lady-killer of independent means. UEA taught me to question standard versions of history. Its abstract concrete was shining new then and the golf course it had been built on was still mourned by the golf-playing classes of Norfolk. While it now even teaches Writing as a business, its 1975 prospectus boasted that it did not train people for any job or profession: that could come after they had been *educated*. Its founding motto, like Norfolk's, was 'Do Different'. UEA was famously full of revolutionary critiques of culture and active left wing students on grants but the largest (if passive) student society was the Federation of Conservative Students, even in those Old Labour days before tuition fees and student loans. My northern comrades next door endured a yacht illegally parked in the window of their study bedroom on which its owner cavalierly paid parking fines as affordable rent.

33. The Ballad of the EAS Rider[17]

Twisting round my hair in knots,
Twisting round your neck with thoughts.
My oh my, you have to agree
Certain issues of poetry
Can't conceive of a harmony.

I'm twisting pastoral flowers into your face.
I'm twisting your kind of thinking into place.
I'm twisting...

Listening to you plum for choice
Between degrees of passive vice.
'There's much that may be said for Donne.'
I am the outside world come in,
Butchered hands and axe grinding,
Open your 'ed and let me in!

I'm twisting pastoral flowers into your face.
I'm twisting your kind of thinking into place.
I'm twisting ....

Your rich aesthetic literariness
Is like the lush grass on a grave.
My oh my I'm rotten through
But life moves through and it's sick – of you.
I'll thrust you off me and trample you.

I'm twisting pastoral flowers into your case
I'm twisting your kind of thinking into place.
I'm ... Terminating this debate!

---

[17]   EAS – The School of English and American Studies, 1977. Punk hits the campus.

34. Yarmouth Visited (A Bingo Blues)

No waiting, no delay,
Jump right in and off we'll play:
On the pink....all alone....number one;
On the yellow....lovely legs....legs eleven....

Money bags busting wind with sand
Weighing the rigs of glitter down,
Bags stuffed sick with golden sand
Weighing the rigs of glitter down.
A tide wheels in between roadside signs,
On sandy fortunes the Gold Disc shines.

On the green....iced scream....sweet sixteen;
On the change....don't be naughty....blind forty....

Dishwasher switches off his tyrants,
Takes a different wavelength;
Miss Radio resists insistent parents,
Takes a different wavelength;
Breakers crash on boundless feelings
Cashed on the rocks of mountainous nothings

On the blue....heaven's gate....fifty eight;
On the grey....at the Styx....sixty six....

Moments are grapes in a heart-crush wine,
Overflowing cups of detail and colour;
Time's cleavage gapes for heart-crush wine,
Overflowing cups of detail and colour,
Infinity collides with the corners of events,
Kaleidoscopic shadows of the One beyond events....

No waiting, no delay,
Jump right in and off we'll play...

35. The Ballad of Wells Next The Sea

Standing in the dock at Hunstanton
Trying to get to Sheringham Sands
The man at the back said
You'll need a big mac,
It's hissing down with rain on the strands.
Crabs! You know it ain't easy
You know how hard it can be,
The way things are going
We're going to Wells next the Sea.

Hired a boat to Burnham Upmarket
Kensington on Overy Staithe.
The nob with the beard said
'Decidedly weird,
The Chablis here don't make any waves.'

Crabs! You know it ain't easy.
You know how hard it can be,
The way things are going,
We're going to Wells next the Sea.

Bridge

Saving up your money for a Cromer crab,
Fish n chips *Hotel de Paris*,
A poet in motion, came out of the Ocean,
The 'Albatros' is where he should be!

Crabs! You know it ain't easy.
You know how hard it can be,
The way things are going,
We're going to Wells next the Sea.

36. The OM of Cromer

Here's the pier we saw Fairport Convention
go down a storm in a blizzard
Of Ghost Ship on ice, with an arctic air-con
scarfing us in the gizzard,

And here's where beach-blonde bikini'd housewives
raise Calypso for a day
Beside that candy-flossed denture smile
of permanent holiday.

And where *Alpha Papa* in the Multiplex
two streets from the real pier
Crosses the line between life and art
over Dis n Styx and a bier

and piers through Edwardian telescopes
at the towers of Troy:
White-hot gulls of summer framed
by the glare of the loneliest boy

Who sprayed his eye with a Right On Guard,
On the run here with a girl
Buttoning her pink heart forever away
As an oyster her precious pearl.

Here: between the rock and roll;
the e-pics and the Homer;
The beach-bum sand and the bottomless sea -
the OM of Cromer.

37. The Ballad of Boal Quay (Lynn)

And when you gave, then turned away, your ocean eyes, I knew
My heart would break in waves there on the rocks of losing you.

I didn't ask for this; I only breathed without belief
Unconscious idle prayers: I never dreamed you'd make them true.

My life's in ruins now; I can't go home, nor to your door:
In bar and hermit chapel, all I taste is missing you.

I talk about you all the time and think I've made some sense
But if my words can't bring you near....what good can they do?

My days were full of waiting for your Christ feet at my door.
They're empty now the dove in hand is just the bird that flew.

You touched me once; I closed my eyes; your warmth was like a fire;
I let it smoulder gently: now it blasts my heart in two.

O lover, don't complain, "this never lost is never found"
The world will think you're crazy and besides it's kind of true.

Tom Conway.

38. The Ballad of Vicky Briton (The Clash With Rome)

Boudica got a lot of Romans
Hanging out in the Styx;
The Woad Goddess goes to school
Where they teach her how to be nix.

She's the Mother of Britain's
Biblical kicks
Against the odds,
Against the pricks.

She's the crazy moon
In a gurly whirl
The finest hour
Of the Norfolk girl!

Ride ride, I wanna ride,
Ride ride, a riot on my horse,
Woad woad, a-whoa woad,
Blow whoa, a riot on my horn!

She's the fury in Janus's office
Sown with the wildest oats,
She's a wild goose-chasing sky,
A whiff of burning boats.

She's the country queen
With the world in sway
Who blooms and blows
It all away.

She's the crazy moon
In a gurly whirl
The finest hour
Of the Norfolk girl!

Ride ride, I wanna ride,
Ride ride, a riot on my horse,
Woad woad, a-whoa woad,
Blow whoa, a riot on my horn!

Anto Morra about to be run down by Boudica's chariot.

39. A Lynn Carol

'This creature had various tokens in her hearing. One was a kind of sound as if it were a pair of bellows blowing in her ear. She – being dismayed at this – was warned in her soul to have no fear, for it was the sound of the Holy Ghost. And then our Lord turned it into the voice of a dove, and afterwards he turned it into the voice of a little bird which is called a redbreast, that often sang very merrily in her right ear.'

The Book of Margery Kempe

'A crown of thorns to freeze your breath
The berried holly brings;
Through snowing sunlight chaste as death
The silent barn-owl wings

But now the ghostly holy dove
That bellows in your ear
Is tuned to robin-song by love
And cheerfully made clear.'

The only gift left on the shelf
That nothing else can rise above
Includes all treasure, lasts forever,
And grows when shared with others: love.

Now starry angels on the tree
Grow larger in the dusk
To heaven-blue and Eden-green
And gold and reindeer-musk.

And what was heard by Margery,
The Visionary of Lynn,
Rings out on tills for checkout girls
Who hear that robin sing.

The only gift left on the shelf,
That nothing else can rise above,
Includes all treasures, lasts forever,
And grows when shared with others: love.

A sacred Ouse of honeyed sound
Above her dreaming bed,
She wakes as one in paradise
And leaps as from the dead.

A thrilling robin in her ear,
A rose that's heaven scent,
A man divine to earthly eye,
All music from Him lent.

The only gift left on the shelf,
That nothing else can rise above,
Includes all treasures, lasts forever,
And grows when shared with others: love.

A Lynn Carol

Gareth Calway

Gillian Sims McLennan

2

rise a-bove In - cludes all trea-sures, lasts_ for - ev- er, And grows when shared with o - thers:_

love._____ 2. Now   love.___ And grows when shared with o -thers:_ love._____

Gillian Sims McLennan

The Ballad of Fiddler's Hill

Gareth Calway

Gill Sims McLennan

1. Ye feast-ers__ up on Fidd-ler's Hill where cross-roads meet the har-row, Take care you don't dis-turb the sleep-ing Bronze Age bu-rial bar-row. O shun this__ ground from dusk till dawn or live a dread-ful tale Of a Black Monk at the tun-nel's mouth to turn your red lips pale. Don't

fol-low the_fidd-ler and his dog to Wal-sing-ham un-der the hill To lay the foul Be-ne

Chorus vv 1 & 2

-dic-tine ghost: that the fidd-ler lays there still. "I will play through the tun-nel"

cried the jol-ly fidd-ler to the cheer-ing lo - cal crowd, "Stamp time and fol-low my

1.2.   3.

tune a - bove, For I play both brave and loud.   chin. "I will

play through the tun-nel" cried the jol-ly fidd-ler and half his boast_ came true "Stamp

rit. (2nd time only)　　　　　**A tempo** (2nd time only)

time and fol-low my tune a-bove!" But he lost them half way through. I will

through.

The Ballad of Fiddlers Hill

Words: Gareth Calway Music: Adrian Tebbutt

INTRO: D G/B   D A7sus4(1) D G/B A7sus4(2) D (x2)

D   **G/B**
You feasters up on Fiddler's Hill
D   **Asus4**
In Binham Priory grounds,
D   **G/B**
Take care you don't disturb the sleeping
A7sus4   **D**
Bronze Age burial mounds.

O shun this ground between dusk and dawn
Or live a dreadful tale
Of a Black Monk at a tunnel's mouth
To turn your red lips pale.

A7   **G/B**
Don't follow the fiddler and his dog
A7sus4   D
To Walsingham under the hill
A7   **G/B**
To lay the foul Benedictine ghost:
A7sus4   D
That fiddler lays there still.

The Fried Pirates

A
"I will play through the tunnel!" said the jolly fiddler
A   G
To the cheering local crowd,
A   G
"Stamp time and follow my tune above,
A7sus4   D
For I play both brave and loud."

D G/B   D A7sus4(1) D G/B A7sus4(2) D

And so he fiddled and so they stamped
His three mile course underground
But his fiddle stopped under Fiddler's Hill
In the silence of the mound.

106

Each dared the next down the tunnel's mouth
But none would dare themselves
And at midnight the fiddler's dog emerged
Like a hound bewitched by the elves.

His tail thrust down between his legs,
His frame a shivering wrack,
He howled and pined at the dreadful hole
But his master never came back.

"I will play through the tunnel!" cried the jolly fiddler
To the cheering local crowd,
"Stamp time and follow my tune above,
For I play both brave and loud."

D G/B D A7sus4(1) D G/B A7sus4(2) D

A violent storm drove everyone home
And when they awoke from sleep
The entrance was gone, the fiddler too,
Into a Nameless Deep.

The moral of this, and it's old as the hill,
Is that mounds aren't for tunnelling,
If a grave tune plucks the strings of your heart,
Keep the devil under your chin.

In this county of beet and barley and beer,
This county of fish and farrow,
There's folk you can trust, there's London folk,
And there's folk who come out of a barrow.

"I will play through the tunnel!" cried the jolly fiddler
And half his boast came true,
"Stamp time and follow my tune above!"
But he lost them half way through.

D G/B D A7sus4(1) D G/B A7sus4(2) D (x2)

Recording information
Adrian Tebbutt: Guitars, Octave and Tenor Mandolins, Vocals

Half God, Half Nelson

Words: Gareth Calway Music: Adrian Tebbutt

Our Admiral's head it has one eye
[A]Heave away! [G]Heave [D]away!
[G]His empty sleeve's the[D] flag we [A]fly.
[G] 'Tell my wife I'm [A]killed,' we [D]say.

[G]*Heave away Hor*[A]*atio's* [D]*boys*
[A]*Heave away!* [G]*Heave* [D]*away!*
[G]*Heave away and make a* [D]*Victory* [A]*noise*
From [G]*Burnham* [A] *to Tr*[G]*afalgar* [D]*bay.*

[G] [D] [A] [D]   [G] [A] [D]

He hunted polar bears, the lad
[A]Heave away! [G]Heave [D]away!
[G] 'To fetch a white rug [D]to my [A]dad.'
[G] 'Tell my wife I'm [A]killed,' we [D]say.

[D]Mosquitoes bit him [G]half to [D]death:
[A]Heave away! [G]Heave [D]away!
'I'll [G] live a hero's [D]life in[A]stead'
[G] 'Tell my wife I'm [A]killed,' we [D]say.

[G]*Heave away Hor*[A]*atio's* [D]*boys*
[A]*Heave away!* [G]*Heave* [D]*away!*
[G]*Heave away and make a* [D]*Victory* [A]*noise*
From [G]*Burnham* [A] *to Tr*[G]*afalgar* [D]*bay.*

[G] [D] [A] [D]   [G] [A] [D]

Off Corsica, his eye foresworn,
[A]Heave away! [G]Heave [D]away!
 [G] 'I got a little [D]hurt this [A]morn.'
[G] 'Tell my wife I'm [A]killed,' we [D]say.

Off [D] Cape St Vincent, [G]breaking [D]ranks,
[A]Heave away! [G]Heave [D]away!
He [G] won the day and [D]England's [A]thanks.
[G] 'Tell my wife I'm [A]killed,' we [D]say.

[G]*Heave away Hor[A]atio's [D]boys*
[A]*Heave away!* [G]*Heave* [D]*away!*
[G]*Heave away and make a* [D]*Victory* [A]*noise*
From [G]*Burnham* [A] *to Tr*[G]*afalgar* [D]*bay.*

[G] [D] [A] [D]   [G] [A] [D]

Our king's right hand at Santa Cruz;
[A]Heave away! [G]Heave [D]away!
A [G] night to seize; an [D]arm to [A]lose.
[G] 'Tell my wife I'm [A]killed,' we [D]say.

'A[D] peerage or [G]Westminster [D]crypt!'
[A]Heave away! [G]Heave [D]away!
He [G] sinks the French down [D]to [A]Egypt
[G] 'Tell my wife I'm [A]killed,' we [D]say.
[G]*Heave away Hor[A]atio's [D]boys*

[A]*Heave away!* [G]*Heave* [D]*away!*
[G]*Heave away and make a* [D]*Victory* [A]*noise*
From [G]*Burnham* [A] *to Tr*[G]*afalgar* [D]*bay.*

[G] [D] [A] [D]   [G] [A] [D]

'Discontinue!' the Admiral flagged
[A]Heave away! [G]Heave [D]away!
[G] 'can't be seen with [D]my eye [A]masked!'
[G] 'Tell my wife I'm [A]killed,' we [D]say.

[D] 'Redoubtable' marks [G] men spy [D]him
[A]Heave away! [G]Heave [D]away!
'They've[G] done for me at [D]last. I'm [A]dying.'

[G] 'Tell my wife I'm [A]killed,' we [D]say.
[G]*Heave away Hor[A]atio's [D]boys*
[A]*Heave away!* [G]*Heave* [D]*away!*
[G]*Heave away and make a* [D]*Victory* [A]*noise*
From [G]*Burnham* [A] *to Tr*[G]*afalgar* [D]*bay.*

[G]*Heave away and make a* [D]*Victory* [A]*noise*
From [G]*Burnham* [D] *to Tr*[A]*afalgar* [D]*bay.*

A Lynn Carol

Words: Gareth Calway Music: Tom Conway

```
    C                 F
'A crown of thorns to freeze your breath
     C           G
The berried holly brings;
        Am              F
Through snowing sunlight chaste as death
     C    Em         D
The silent barn-owl wings
```

```
     Dm           C
But now the ghostly holy dove
      C      F      G
That bellows in your ear
     F            C
Is tuned to robin-song by love
        G  Dm      G     G Dm G   G Dm G
And cheerfully made clear.'
```

```
    C                 F
The only gift left on the shelf
       C            G
That nothing else can rise above
  Am                    F
Includes all treasure, lasts forever,
       C                        Em    D
And grows when shared with others: love.
```

Lightning Source UK Ltd.
Milton Keynes UK
UKOW07f1051241115

263427UK00001B/15/P